3/18

OUTDOOR EXPLORERS

Southeast

Helen Foster James

Published in the United States of America
by Cherry Lake Publishing
Ann Arbor, Michigan
www.cherrylakepublishing.com

Reading Adviser: Marla Conn MS, Ed., Literacy specialist, Read-Ability, Inc.

Photo Credits: © FatCamera / iStockphoto.com, cover, 1; © Chayanin Wongpracha / Shutterstock.com, 6 ; ©PHOTO MALETIC / Shutterstock.com, 8, 12; © jthomasweb / Shutterstock.com, 10; © Florist Kuniko / Shutterstock.com, 10; ©James Laurie / Shutterstock.com, 11; © Nikolay Kurzenko / Shutterstock.com, 11; © Danielle Davis Reports / Shutterstock.com, 12; © PAKULA PIOTR / Shutterstock.com, 13; © Skyprayer2005 / Shutterstock.com, 13; © Ron Rowan Photography / Shutterstock.com, 14, 19; © Birute Vijeikiene / Shutterstock.com, 16; © evenfh / Shutterstock.com, 16; © Tom Grundy / Shutterstock.com, 17; © John A. Anderson / Shutterstock.com, 17; © Jason Patrick Ross / Shutterstock.com, 18; © Kat Grant Photographer / Shutterstock.com, 18; © Jim Cumming / Shutterstock.com, 19; © Roman023_photography / Shutterstock.com, 20; © wavebreakmedia / Shutterstock.com, 20; © Kingcraft / Shutterstock.com, 20; © India Picture / Shutterstock.com, 20; © Bram Reusen / Shutterstock.com, 22; © Jon Bilous / Shutterstock.com, 22; © Romrodphoto / Shutterstock.com, 22; © Photo Image / Shutterstock.com, 22

Library of Congress Cataloging-in-Publication Data
Names: James, Helen Foster, 1951- author.
Title: Southeast / Helen Foster James.
Description: Ann Arbor : Cherry Lake Publishing, 2017. |
    Series: Outdoor explorers | Includes bibliographical references
    and index. | Audience: Grades K to 3.
Identifiers: LCCN 2016057051| ISBN 9781634728751 (hardcover) |
    ISBN 9781634729642 (pdf) | ISBN 9781534100534 (pbk.) |
    ISBN 9781534101425 (hosted ebook)
Subjects: LCSH: Natural history—Southern States—Juvenile literature.
Classification: LCC QH104.5.S59 J36 2017 | DDC 508.75—dc23
LC record available at https://lccn.loc.gov/2016057051

Cherry Lake Publishing would like to acknowledge the work of the Partnership for 21st Century Skills. Please visit www.p21.org for more information.

Printed in the United States of America
Corporate Graphics

Table of Contents

WASHINGTON

MONTANA

NORTH DAKOTA

M

OREGON

IDAHO

WYOMING

SOUTH DAKOTA

NEBRASKA

NEVADA

UTAH

COLORADO

KANSAS

CALIFORNIA

ALASKA

ARIZONA

NEW MEXICO

OKLAHOMA

TEXAS

HAWAII

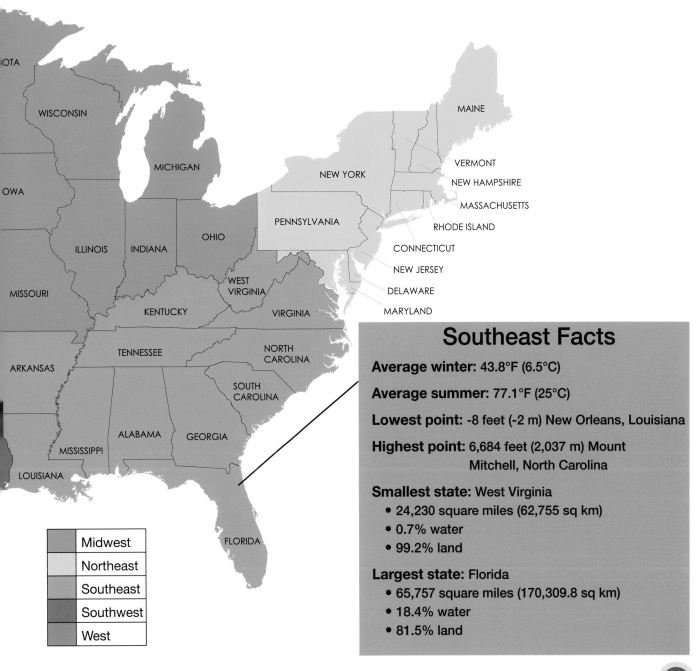

WISCONSIN

MICHIGAN

IOWA

OTA

ILLINOIS INDIANA OHIO

NEW YORK

PENNSYLVANIA

MAINE

VERMONT

NEW HAMPSHIRE

MASSACHUSETTS

RHODE ISLAND

CONNECTICUT

NEW JERSEY

DELAWARE

MARYLAND

MISSOURI

KENTUCKY

WEST
VIRGINIA

VIRGINIA

ARKANSAS

TENNESSEE

NORTH
CAROLINA

SOUTH
CAROLINA

MISSISSIPPI

ALABAMA GEORGIA

LOUISIANA

FLORIDA

Midwest
Northeast
Southeast
Southwest
West

Southeast Facts

Average winter: 43.8°F (6.5°C)

Average summer: 77.1°F (25°C)

Lowest point: -8 feet (-2 m) New Orleans, Louisiana

Highest point: 6,684 feet (2,037 m) Mount
Mitchell, North Carolina

Smallest state: West Virginia
- 24,230 square miles (62,755 sq km)
- 0.7% water
- 99.2% land

Largest state: Florida
- 65,757 square miles (170,309.8 sq km)
- 18.4% water
- 81.5% land

It's time for a nature hike.
Let's see what we can see.

Mississippi's official state tree is the southern magnolia tree. It doesn't lose its leaves in the fall. Why do you think this is?

Plants

I see a magnolia tree. Its leaves are smooth and shiny.

Tall palm trees reach for the sky. The leaves are up high. They are shaped like fans.

I see pine trees. I feel and smell the **bark**. I collect the **pinecones**.

American Beautyberry

- This shrub produces pink flowers and purple berries.

- The leaves can be used as insect repellent.

Cherokee Rose

- Georgia's official state flower since 1916.

- This bush can be found climbing over other plants.

Louisiana Iris

- Louisiana's official state wildflower since 1990.

- This plant can be found by lakes, ponds, and swamps.

Pine Tree

- North Carolina's official state tree since 1963.

- Some pine trees grow up to 150 feet (45.7 meters) tall; others only grow up to 4 feet (1 m).

Sabal Palm Tree

- Florida's official state tree since 1953.

- The leaves can be as long as 12 feet (3.6 m) and as wide as 6 feet (1.8 m).

Southern Magnolia Tree

- The flowers can be as wide as 12 inches (30 centimeters).

- This tree keeps most of its leaves all year.

Sweetshrub

- This bush can grow up to 10 feet (3 m).

- The dried leaves and flowers can make a room smell nice.

Yellow Jessamine

- South Carolina's official state flower since 1924.

- The entire plant is poisonous to humans and many animals.

The northern mockingbird is the official state bird of Florida, Tennessee, Mississippi, Arkansas, and Texas.
Which of these states are in the Southeast?

Animals

I listen carefully for a mockingbird. I hear it singing.

I see a deer and her fawn. The fawn has white spots. Maybe I'll also see a bat flying.

What animals would you like to see on your nature hike?

American Alligator

- Official state reptile of Florida, Louisiana, and Mississippi.

- These reptiles are fast in water and slow on land.

American Black Bear

- West Virginia's official state animal since 1973.

- It is the smallest bear found in the United States.

Big-eared Bat

- Virginia's official state bat since 2005.

- Its flexible ears are about half the length of its 4 inch (10 cm) body.

Eastern Box Turtle

- Official state reptile of North Carolina and Tennessee.

- They can live over 100 years.

Green Tree Frog

- Official state amphibian of Georgia and Louisiana.

- These big-eyed animals can grow a little over 2 inches (5 cm).

Northern Cardinal

- Official state bird of Kentucky, North Carolina, Virginia, and West Virginia.

- The male and female take turns feeding their baby birds.

Northern Mockingbird

- Their long tail feathers are about the length of their body.

- The male can learn about 200 different songs.

White-tailed Deer

- South Carolina's official state animal since 1972.

- The color of their coat, or fur, changes with the season.

Spring

Summer

Fall

Winter

Weather

The air feels warm during spring.
I pick the wildflowers growing.

It is **humid** in summer. I sit in the
shade. I find shapes in the clouds.

I like hiking in fall. It's not too hot.

It snows in some places during winter.
In other places it rains.

Mountain

Ocean

Swamp

River

Geography

I hike through the mountains. I draw the many trees.

I take photos of the **Atlantic Ocean**. The water is cold. The waves look strong.

I study the swamp. I see a carpet of green plants floating in it.

I write down what I see by the river. The river rocks feel smooth.

Where would you like to hike?

Find Out More

Gillis, Jennifer Blizin. *The Southeast*. Chicago: Raintree, 2006.

Marsico, Katie. *It's Cool to Learn about the United States: Southeast (Social Studies Explorer)*. Ann Arbor: Cherry Lake Publishing, 2012.

Glossary

amphibian (am-FIB-ee-uhn) a cold-blooded animal that lives in water and breathes with gills when young; as an adult, it develops lungs and lives on land

Atlantic Ocean (uht-LAN-tik OH-shuhn) the world's second-largest ocean; it borders the eastern United States

bark (BAHRK) the tough covering on the stems of shrubs, trees, and other plants

humid (HYOO-mid) moist and very warm in a way that is uncomfortable

insect repellent (IN-seckt ri-PEL-uhnt) a chemical that wards off insects

pinecones (PINE-kohnz) hard and dry parts that are the fruit of a pine tree and contain many seeds

poisonous (POI-zuh-nuhs) having a poison that can harm or kill

reptile (REP-tile) a cold-blooded animal with scaly, dry skin that crawls across the ground or creeps on short legs

swamps (SWAHMP) areas of wet, spongy ground

Index

About the Author

Helen Foster James is a volunteer interpretive naturalist for her local state park. She lives by the ocean and loves to hike in the mountains. She is the author of *S Is for S'mores: A Camping Alphabet* and more than 20 other books for children.